COMMERCIAL SPACE

Offices, Design and Layout

COMMERCIAL SPACE

Offices, Design and Layout

RotoVision SA

AUTHOR
Francisco Asensio Cerver

EDITOR IN CHIEF
Paco Asensio

PROJECT COORDINATOR
Rosa Maria Prats

PROOFREADING
Tobias Willett

TRANSLATION
A.B.C. Traduccions

© Copyright for international edition
AXIS BOOKS, S.A.

© Copyright for English edition
ROTOVISION

ISBN: 2-88046-251-7

To confront the concepts of interior design or interior architecture is an arduous task in which any absolute judgement may founder in a spectacular fashion against the heterogeneous and changing reality of the contemporary creative panorama. To confine this enormous territory within the sphere of public activities further complicates this approach to a phenomenon which arises as the logical consequence of the individual's needs to socialise. Habitual and common aspects of human behaviour are likewise subject to constant modifications which, expressed as tendencies, currents or fashions, arise with the same rapidity as they disappear.

The selection of premises which we present here could be considered a compendium of the spaces which have managed, with greater or lesser good fortune, to introduce themselves into such difficult markets as work, wielding the weapons of originality, innovation, and an undeniable passion for the world of architecture and design. The projects exhibited here are a reflection of a short period in social and chronological history in which new concepts and tendencies have appeared already superposed and overlapping, and not as the consequence of an exclusive dialectic or for concrete reasons.

On the other hand, the rationalisation and bureaucratisation of the world of work demands spaces endowed with qualitative dignity in which employees can perform their labour pleasantly and efficiently.

The separation of the home and the professional environment has converted contemporary life into a constant itinerary which takes the individual from his private sphere (the home) to the semi-private domain (the office). Between these two extremes, the need for socialisation has brought with it an emphasis on and the resurgence of certain spaces which, whilst traditionally present, have now acquired more complex values and a greater intrinsic richness.

The offices presented in this volume correspond to work areas which are either partially or totally in contact with the public, and refer especially to the design of offices and financial or administrative headquarters. The interest that experimentation in this field has awoken in recent years is the logical consequence of the function these spaces have of attracting or alluring in a commercial or representative sense. The culture of image has become a new value, turning company buildings into reflections of the spirit of their work, and the work done on them is considered as an investment which will soon yield a profit.

Offices, Design and Layout

OFFICES, DESIGN AND LAYOUT

JARDINE HOUSE

Eva Jiricna & Michael Hopkins

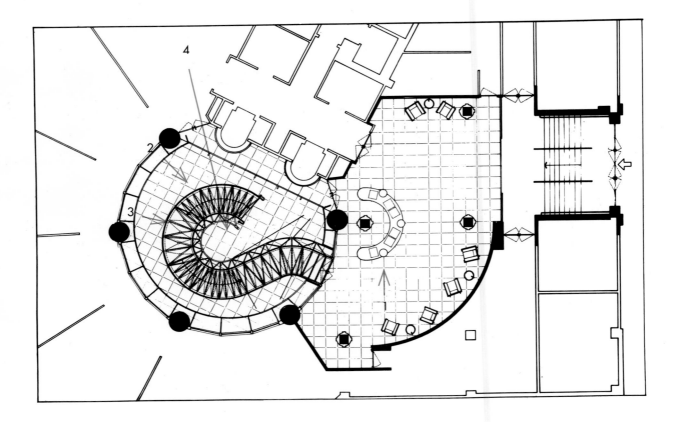

Floor plan of the Jardine Insurance Company building, with the particular distribution of the space surrounding the principal areas: the entrance and reception area, and the central atrium.

A partial view of the reception area, with the round counter designed by Eva Jiricna, its structure encircling one of the four cylindrical columns. (1)

A view, from one of the upper levels of the building, of the atrium and the foot of the great stairway which leads to the different offices and rooms. The curvilinear design of the ornamental elements and the furniture further emphasises the predominance of sinuous structures which is so characteristic of the interior of the building. (2)

This joint project taken on by the architectural studios of Eva Jiricna and Michael Hopkins to do the design work for a number of emblematic spaces in an office building in London, perfectly exemplifies the interdependent nature of interior design and architecture. The work was limited to the design of a series of interiors which had to reflect the corporate identity of the client, the Jardine Insurance Company. The most outstanding achievements of Jiricna and Hopkins, with regard to this project, were the system of internal communications, the layout of the functional areas and the definition of the work areas, where a rational division of the space was imposed in order to take maximum advantage of the natural light. The final result is an elegant combination of materials, colours and curvilinear forms which merges the sophistication of high-technology with a sensitive interpretation of the possibilities offered by the existing space.

In 1963 Eva Jiricna graduated from the Architecture and Urban Studies Faculty of the University of Prague, in 1990, after several years working for the Interior Design Institute in Prague, for the GLC Schools Division (England) and in the Louis de Soisons' practice she became associated with David Hodges, with whom she worked in London on the designs for Le Caprice Restaurant, a Kenzo boutique and an apartment in Chelsea. In 1985 after several years as a consultant architect she set up her own practice, Eva Jiricna Architects, producing designs for Harrod's, Joe's Cafe, Esprit and Comme Ci Comme Ca, among other clients.

Michael Hopkins graduated in architecture in 1963 and, from 1969 to 1975, he worked for Foster Associates before joining the Patty Hopkins firm in 1986. He has also worked

A perspective of the atrium from behind the staircase illustrating the radial structure of the different rooms, laid out around the axis formed by the staircase itself. (3)

with John Pringle, Ian Sharrat and Bill Taylor. Among his most outstanding projects are the Greene King Brewery in Bury St. Edmunds, an educational centre for IBM in London, the Schlumberger Research Centre in Cambridge and a project for the Victoria and Albert Museum, also in London.

The principal aim of the design for the Jardine House company was to impose a memorable and distinctive corporate image on selected areas of the premises which would emphasise the identity of the company. The work, limited to the most important public areas, had three main focuses: the entrance and reception area; the central atrium, featuring a singular staircase leading to the four executive dining rooms; and a conference

A detail of the metallic structure of the main stairway and, on the page opposite, a spectacular perspective of the atrium from the top floor of the building. The radial distribution is clearly shown, with the different offices laid out at different height levels around a central axis, interconnected by the staircase, and by lifts from the ground floor. (4)

Different aspects of the conference room on the top floor, with its glass dome, allowing for the permeation of natural light during the day. A high technology mechanism controls the protective screen located under the dome, which closes in order to control the possible excess of light (see previous page).

room, on the top floor. The overall guidelines for the project: effectiveness, transparency and seriousness, were imposed in response to the need to create a specific, and unified, corporate identity for the Jardine company.

The most innovative forms, technical applications and materials were employed for the interior design, both in terms of layout and the different functional and ornamental elements. The sinuous configuration of some of these elements, particularly the impressive staircase leading up from the ground floor of the central atrium, also reflect the fidelity of the two architects to the most up to date creative tendencies.

The preexisting volumetric characteristics had a decisive influence on the interior design. The structure is articulated around a vertical cylindrical space, surrounded by curved sequence of wall facings, organised around circular columns. This particular layout, based on curved lines, finds its strongest expression in the reception area, through the radial distribution of the offices and in the room on the top floor with its glazed dome.

The architects managed to adapt their creative capacity, and their design for this space, to the special geometry of the building, dominated by curves; and also to the objectives of the client, which required that the offices should reflect the corporate image of the company. Jiricna and Hopkins have achieved a stylish execution of great elegance through a synthesis of the most contemporary aspects of modern design and a sensitive interpretation of the company image.

On this and the previous page, various perspectives and details of the metallic structure of the main staircase.

UNIFOR

Afra Bianchin & Tobia Scarpa

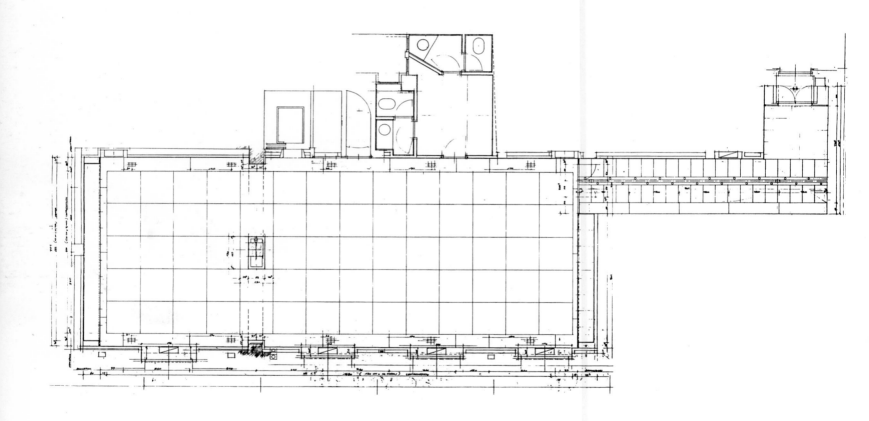

Floor plan of the lower level of the building, destined for offices and washrooms.

On the following page, a view of the ground floor showing, on the left, the giant table which dominates the space. This simply designed object functions both as a decorative element and as a display counter for different pieces from the Unifor collection which are exhibited on the table fully, visible to the public from the entrance to the premises.

The Unifor Showroom in Milan, the work of the Venetian architects Afra Bianchin and Tobia Scarpa, serves as an expression of the architects' singular conception of their craft as a discipline which defines a spatial order that reserves a place for other art forms and their aesthetic content.

Both of these architect/designers graduated from the Institute of Architecture of the University of Venice and started working together after completing their studies. In 1960 they became associated with Gavina, designing pieces such as the Bastiano divan and the Vanessa bed, both currently exhibited in the Knoll International Collection. They also designed a collection of domestic furniture for Cassina, some of the pieces of which are part of the permanent collection of the Museum of Modern Art in New York. They worked with Flos, alongside Achille Castiglione, designing the Papillona standard lamp and the Pierrot table lamp. They have both also worked with Maxalto, Stildomus, Molteni, Unifor and other important companies working in the office furniture sector. The corporate image of Benetton and some of its principle European and American studios are also the work of Bianchin and Scarpa. Their most important architectural projects include the restoration of various houses, including the Minelli and Fragiacomo villas in Trieste and the Casa di Risparmio in Reggio nell'Emilia.

The project for Unifor reflects the tendency of the architects to determine the spatial order through the application of other formal arts. In

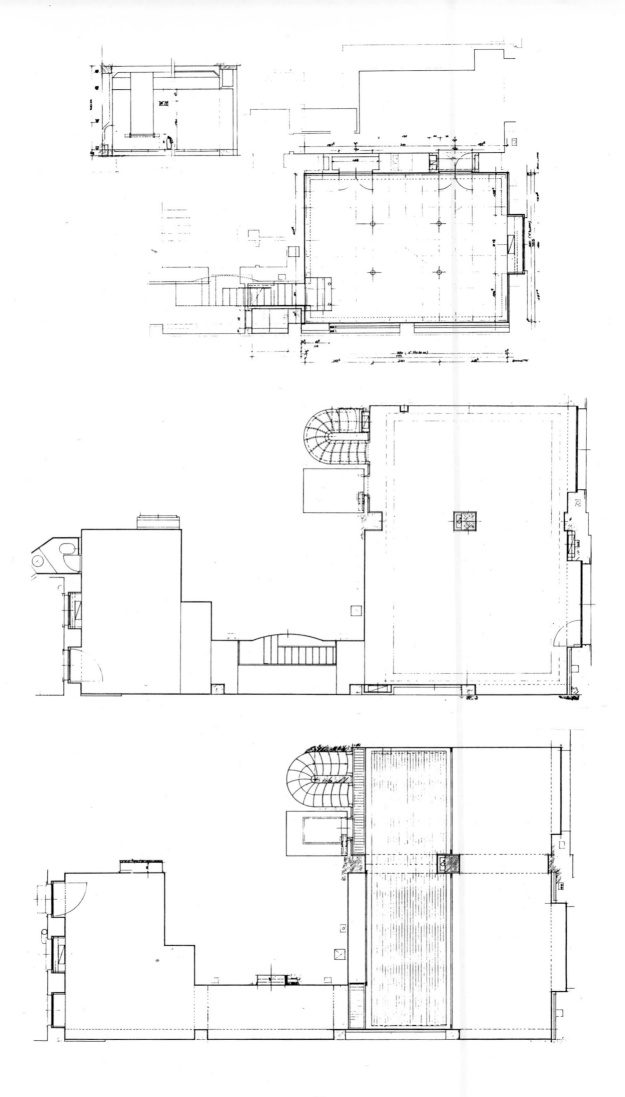

On the page opposite, floor plans of the different levels of the premises, starting with the reception area (above), and moving on to the top floor, divided in two by the large platform.

On this page, above, a view of one of the spaces destined for the display of the furniture collections and, below, a detail of the steep stairs which lead from the entrance to the lower level.

particular Bianchin and Scarpa make extensive use of ornamentation, taking into account the two semantic values of the term, referring to both the aesthetic significance and the social (recognition of and order). The interior of this space must be considered as the container of everyday elements, to which life is imparted by the material and ornamental quality of the walls which enclose them. The architects have developed a series of discreet stylistic symbols articulated throughout the premises, which instill character into the different spaces.

The premises consist of three volumetrically diverse levels brought together by a colour scheme incorporating bands of pastel shading which decorate the white walls in the style of cornices. The lower level, reached by means of a red marble stairway, holds the toilet area. At street level there is a small space which serves as a reception and distributional area. Access to the first floor is by means of another stairway, featuring a design that emphasises the vertical perspective, and which has allowed the addition of a kind of platform serving as an additional level to increasing the available display space.

The chromatic treatment serves as an ornamental element of the highest quality, which significantly contributes to the perception of the internal distribution of the space. The colour schemes and the lighting are mutually complementary, sketching in warm and attractive spaces and ambiences, which become decorative components of great importance.

The simplicity of the materials used contributes to the extension of the expressive capacity of the interior design. In Unifor the classical Venetian decorative concept is subtly reinterpreted and adapted to modern day trends. The

A perspective of the platform located on the upper level, which allows for the increase of the available display area. The chromatic treatment of the walls is one of the characteristic notes of the space, with a predominance of pastel shades contributing to the creation of a subdued and pleasant atmosphere

traditional materials, such as marble, terracotta, and others, have a discreet presence which nevertheless imposes a characteristic note on the atmosphere as a whole. The walls are clad with a special mixture of marble and lime providing a matt finish to the surfaces, still manage, however, to maintain their luminous presence. The terrazzo flooring is finished with a type of tile work based on lime and small white and black pebbles, reminiscent of traditional Venetian ceramic tiles, and is decorated with various ornamental motifs.

The work of Bianchin and Scarpa on this commercial space in Milan is a perfect example of the fusion of diverse artistic disciplines at the service of a spatial organisation based on the effectiveness of the detail work and the

design concept. The use of traditional materials and techniques does not interfere with the commercial objectives of the premises; on the contrary, it has favoured the creation of a space where the design quality of the furniture on display is allowed to predominate in a beautiful yet, at the same time, discreet environment which also functions as an ideal workplace for the company's staff.

Above, a partial view of the area set aside for offices and washrooms, on the lower level of the premises.

On the page opposite, a view of the platform on the upper floor, with the picture windows which are a feature of the glazed façade and, below, a detail of the flooring on the ground floor, characterised by an unusual composition reminiscent of antique Venetian tile work.

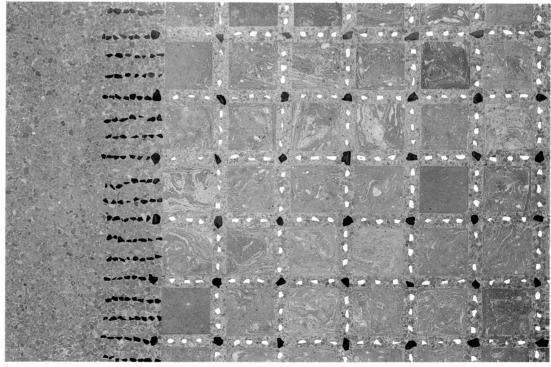

27

On the page opposite, above, a view of the stairway which leads from the reception to the basement level; below, a detail plan of the colour scheme of the walls, based on pastel shades.

On this page, two views of the entrance area, with the stairs leading to the upper level of the premises.

COMP 14

Mario Foltran & Nerino Meneghello

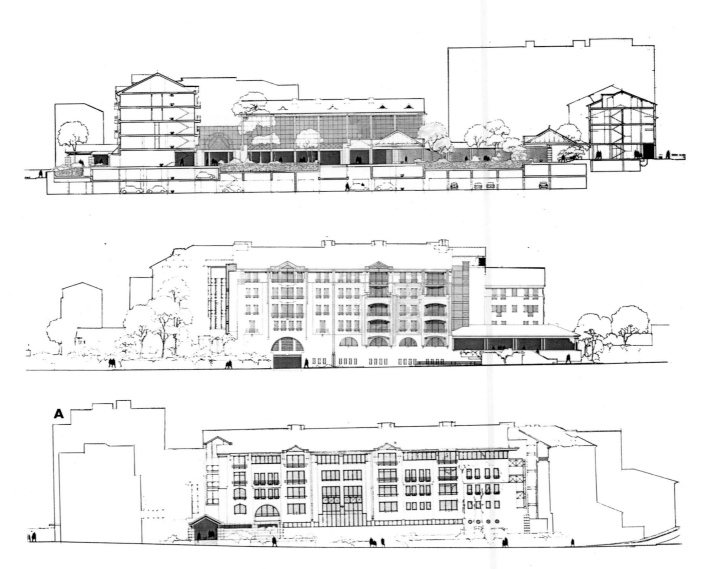

Elevation plan of the façades of the different buildings which make up the complex.

Above, a view of one of the main façades (A) and, below, a perspective of the arch in the interior quadrangle, notable for its metallic profiles and for the upper surface, clad in reflecting glass.

In 1990 the Italian architects Mario Foltran and Nerino Meneghello received recognition of their work with the International Award for Innovative Technology in Architecture, awarded for an architectural and town planning project for the rehabilitation of part of the historic town centre of Conegliano. The project was articulated around the magnificent remodelling of an office complex which, in addition to the strictly

functional aspect (commercial premises, offices, dwellings and parking area), contributed other qualitative, aesthetic and, above all, urban planning values which have converted it into one of the most representative spaces in the city.

Foltran and Meneghello graduated in architecture from the University of Venice and have worked as associates since 1966. The principle focus of their work is public and private construction, town planning, industrial design and interior decoration. Their long careers have been marked by outstanding work including: a variety of buildings for industrial companies in Belluno, Verona, Bolzano, Treviso and Turin; residential complexes and family dwellings in Treviso and Verona; schools and cultural centres in Conegliano and Montebelluna; religious buildings in a great many different localities; office buildings in Belluno, Verona, Padua, Pieve di Soligo and Treviso; sports installations and hospital; and finally the restoration of historic monuments in Conegliano, Treviso and Sacile. In recent years they have developed and directed projects for the rebuilding of historic centres and urban landscapes in Grado, Bardolino, Peschiera, and other Italian towns and cities.

The main aim of the Conegliano project was the recuperation and rebuilding of an area of the town which had been a centre of

A perspective of one of the arcades, with a variety of commercial spaces and shops distributed along its length.

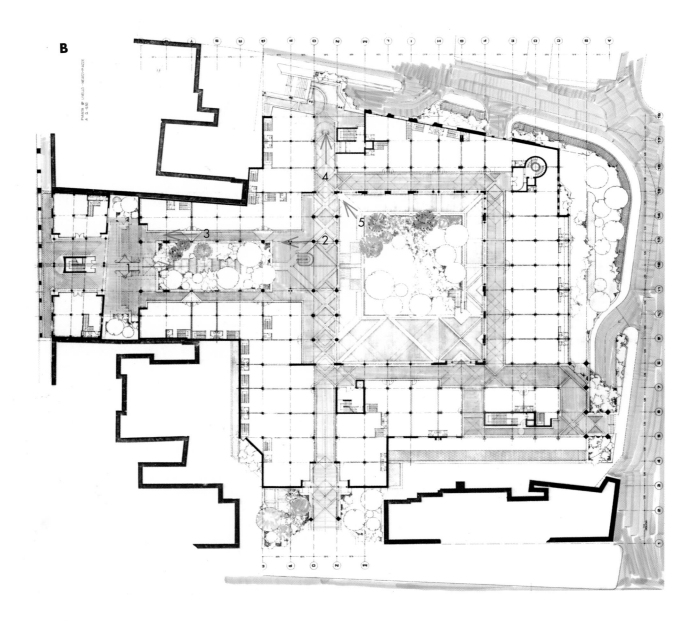

B

industrial activity until the beginning of the 20th century. The plan of action was based on concepts of movement and spatial dynamics, factors which would allow the complex to achieve a fitting correspondence between the interior and the exterior, and would provide a natural system of communications and, consequently, an optimum return. Foltran and Meneghello established a brilliant understanding of the urban and environmental needs, in which both plastic and strictly utilitarian elements were combined. This fusion was achieved through the implementation of the most innovative technology and traditional craftsman's methods, in order to dramatise a series of internal routes which would allow

Floor plan of Comp14, the buildings of which are laid out as an enclosure around a quadrangle, surrounded by arcades and passageways which link the different areas. (B)

A perspective of the main green area, from one of the arcades. (B1)

the rich variety of forms, materials and colour schemes to be perceived within a pleasant environment, appropriate for commercial as well as working and residential functions.

The different buildings, both residential and offices, are laid out in the form of an enclosure in order to give shape to a quadrangle which physically and visually oxygenate the complex. A perpendicular passageway was added to this space completing the framework of interior relationships.

The two basement floors were set aside for parking facilities and a storage area. Almost 2,800 m² of space for commercial activities were distributed in the perimeter streets, and another 4,100 for the housing of a varied interior system of arcades, squares and green areas

corresponding to the spaces which would physically relate the different constructive bodies.

With regard to the façades, the differentiation that was established between the exterior elevations, opening out onto the perimeter streets, and the interior façades are worthy of mention. The former are the result of a basic remodelling work which has respected the essence of the original architecture, without renouncing the use of modern techniques and materials. The prismatic forms of the building are complemented by aluminium profiles, hidden from view, clearances for ventilation and structural insulation. Surfaces areas, such as the balconies with their curved railings, have a base of coloured borders which give a visual organisation to the design of the façades, this sober and elegant composition is complemented by the plasticity of the lines formed by the tinted translucent glass, the mechanistic work-

Perspective of one of the passageways, with various shops distributed along its length (B2), on the following page, another view of the surrounding arcade which runs round the interior garden area. (B3)

ing of the angles of the construction, the brass spacers and the mouldings.

Internally the façades have been given a treatment based on continuous planes of structural glass. The ridged figures acquire a notable relevance, both in terms of the elevations and the layouts of the different arcades. An extended arch of metallic profiles, completely clad in reflecting glass, emerges from a rectangular surface formed of wooden battens, and overlooks the interior quadrangle.

The green areas distributed throughout the enclosure are totally integrated into the archi-

A partial view of one of the glazed porches forming part of the systems for linking the different parts of the complex.

tectural composition, breathing life into the interior of the complex. The arcades and glazed areas create spaces in which a relaxing and restful environment is generated.

Foltran and Meneghello, through their remodelling work on this part of the historic centre of Conegliano, have achieved their principle objective of a dignified recuperation of a public urban space. The project was conceived as an internal tour, whereby the passer through would be able to enjoy the variety and richness of each of the different sectors, commercial, residential and offices.

A view of the extensive interior quadrangle seen from one of the entrance porticos.

On the previous page, a view of one of the arcades, facing the exterior, and illustrating the original glazed structure which covers these corridors, with the tubular steel and iron spars which frame the transparent glass. (B4)

Above, another perspective of the same arcade, from the interior quadrangle (B5), below, a detail of the columns and pillars which support the structures of the roofs of the arcades and corridors.

INVEST CATALANA
"THE MONEY SHOP"

Josep Samsó & Pilar Vila

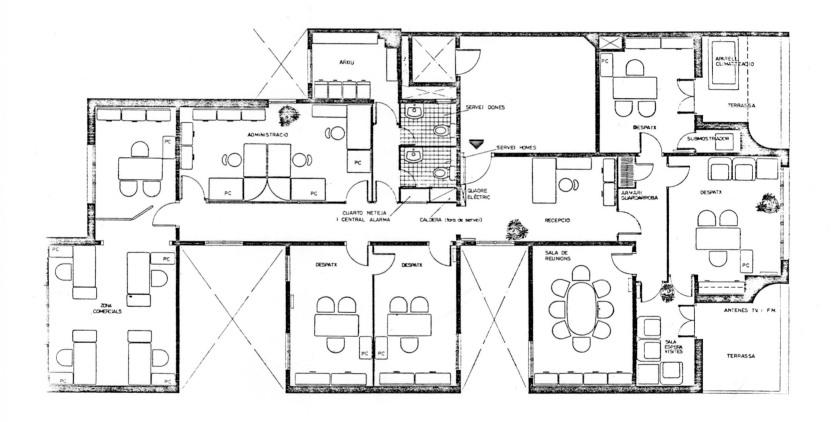

Floor plan of the interior services area, with the rational layout of the offices, board and meeting rooms, and other spaces.

The main façade with the entrance.

A partial view of the central domed area and one of the pillars, with the TV screens in the background. (1)

A view of the dome, with the consultation booths to the left. (2)

The project by Samsó and Vila for the office of this Barcelona bank is an exercise in interior architecture which takes full advantage of a rigorous organisation and spatial hierarchy.

Josep Samsó began his career in architecture in the offices of the architects Bohigas, Martorell and Mackay, where he worked for 15 years. After his experience with this prestigious architectural firm he set up his own architecture and engineering practice together with Francesc Albardané and Laura Takahashi. The Banca Catalana, in Barcelona's Avenida Diagonal; the headquarters of Wang España, S.A.; and the technical and financial supervision of the work on the Palau San Jordi, in Barcelona are among his most outstanding projects. Pilar Vila studied interior design and draughtsmanship and, since 1978, has worked for the Banca Catalana, drawing up technical reports on the selection of suitable premises and carrying out the interior design work for the bank.

To a great extent the refurbishing work on these premises is hidden by the design elements around which the space is distributed. The decorative and sign elements include a unit of laser beams, television screens and a Video-wall. The mezzanine and basement levels of the old premises have been integrated into the overall space, the former becoming an office in which the customers are attended, and the latter an area of internal services. Both of these spaces are visually linked with the rest of the interior by means of the vertical glazed wall surfaces of the stairway.

The old cast-iron pillars, located in the central area are visually linked by a dome which is lit by fibre optics and which radially divides

Above, a partial view of the stairs which leads from the ground floor to the office for attending to the clients located on what was the mezzanine level of the original premises. (3)

A view of one of the consultation booths. (4)

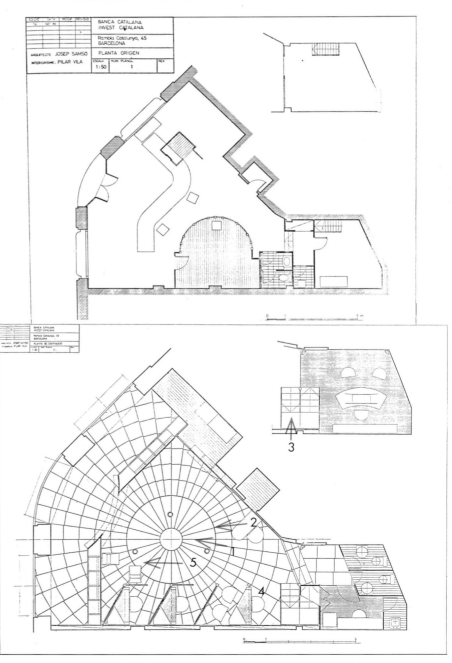

the surface area of the roof, along the lines established by the floor.

Specially designed, perforated metal sheeting and sand blasted glass, painted with Ferrobrun paint, have been used on the surfaces and for the wall cladding. Volcanic rock enamelled in shades of iridescent blue have been used for the flooring, and an iridescent shade of black for the surfaces of the tables and the panels which separate the different consultation booths.

In brief, this remodelling of a space which is both aesthetically pleasing and functional, as defined by the needs of the bank, has also managed to achieve a pleasant and elegant working environment.

On the page opposite, above, another perspective of the ground floor, seen from one of the small consultation rooms. Below, floor plans of the original premises and the new layout.

A view of the small consultation booths, separated by metallic dividing partitions. (5)

RSB BÜROGEBÄUDE

Ernst Giselbrecht

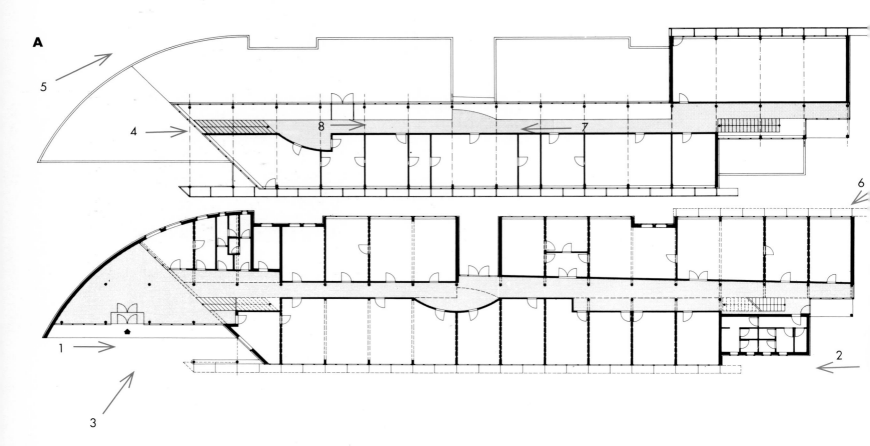

Floor plan of the building, above, the upper and, below, the lower levels. Both levels are laid out on two surfaces of a rectangular geometry, although they are different in terms of size and shape.

On the following page, a view of the two entrances to the complex; above, the principal entrance (A1) and, below, the secondary entrance (A2).

The RSB building in the Austrian town of Voralberg, is the head office of the Rundstahlbau company, a worldwide company specialising in casings for rotating bodies. One of the principal aims of the construction work on this complex was that it should interact with its surroundings in order to modify and redistribute the space in relation to the existing components which defined it. The building also had to respond to a strict functionality, without rejecting technical and human needs, to create an ideal and transparent environment which would faithfully reflect the image of the company. The project presents a combination of the most up to date technical, constructive and material strategies which, as well as offering a modern and progressive image, also met the client's requirement for a rapid execution.

The project architect, Erns Giselbrecht, studied at the Technical University of Graz, and as early as 1978, while he was still attending the university, had already received both the International UIA Competition prize in Mexico, and the Karl Scheffel Memorial Prize. Throughout his professional career his work has been shown in numerous exhibitions, including those in Vienna, New York, Berlin, Mexico, Kassel, Cologne, Hamburg, Bolzano, Bologna, Genoa and Edinburgh.

A perspective of the northern façade, with a functional aesthetic suited to the industrial area which it overlooks, and characterised by the use of glazing and the angled metal roof supports. (A3)

B

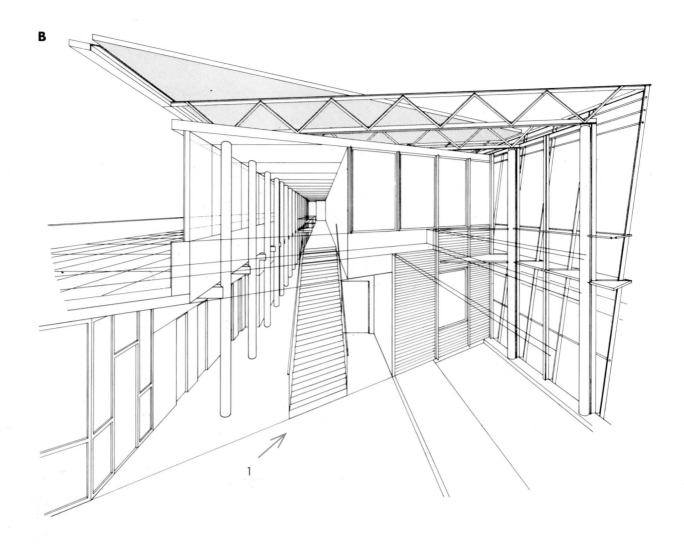

An elevation section of the main foyer, featuring by a stairway which leads to the first floor passageway giving access to the different rooms. (B)

His work has also been awarded many prizes, including, in recent years, four first prizes: for the competition to present a project for a multi-functional centre in Köflach; for the extension of a school and its gymnasium in St.Peter/Judenburg; and for the creation of the Strass Popular School and the Kärnten Doctors House in Klagenfurt. Giselbrecht has imparted his architectural knowledge at a variety of conferences and seminars, expressing his ideas concerning the realisation of projects, and has also represented Austrian architecture at a number of international forums.

Within its urban context the complex had to be built in such a way that it would redefine a landscape dominated by the industrial

An aerial view of the building, with the main entrance in the foreground.

sector of the company itself and by a contingent area of natural beauty which would have to be used for dwellings. The building had to mediate between these two spaces and this resulted in a distinct treatment being applied to the two façades, facing in one direction or the other. The building thus fulfils a double finality, the space of the intervention being converted into the receptor of visual perspectives of great beauty and, at the same time, assuming the function of the focus of images which contribute to the establishment of a new definition of a landscape which had, previously, consisted of two sectors of conflicting aesthetics and configurations. The RSB building, due to its diagonal division, is seen as marking the separation between these two

contiguous spaces, and yet it functions as a nexus of union, through its presentation of a duality of external appearances, reflecting the dual nature of its surroundings.

The complex houses administrative and technical services spaces, such as the technical drawing and draughting rooms. The functional nucleus is distributed on two rectangular floors with a series of contiguous installations which contribute to the formalizing of a floor plan of a highly irregular tendency. The two floors present differences in terms of size and shape, with the consequent superimposition of volumes, and feature terraces of a varied design.

The curvature of the site is a response to the disposition of the foyer, which occupies the first floor and is defined in terms of a section of a circumference. The adjacent washrooms are located on the western flank,

Access from the upper floor to the flat roof, with magnificent panoramic views of the surrounding landscape, including green areas of great natural beauty. (A4)

Another perspective of the main entrance to the building.

formed by two prismatic modules which project beyond the floor plan. These modules are
established in terms of their ends, sketching a
composition of planes and bodies of distinct
heights and layouts.

The process of distribution is articulated
around the strategic layout of passageways
and accesses which seek not only to connect
the different spaces, but also to impose the
maximum clarity and luminosity on the interi-
or spaces.

The building is, finally, resolved on the
basis of an exterior treatment which links it to
the two areas which constitute the duality of its
setting, the residential and the industrial sectors. It serves to separate these two areas,
while at the same time acting as a nexus for

A view of the building's southern façade overlooking the
contiguous residential area, the façade consists of undulat-
ing aluminium cladding complemented by a systematic
layout of volumetric interruptions on the ground floor,
with the glazed gallery above. (A5)

the bringing together and reinterpretation of the landscape as a whole on the basis of certain fundamental urban concepts. The constructive techniques employed in this project are developed with great effectiveness and economy, in response to the requirement for a rapid execution which was one of the most important conditioners of the project. The audacity which is evident in certain aspects of the structural design contributes to the avant-garde image which has converted this building into a faithful and communicative statement of the image required by the company.

A perspective of the lateral and south facing façades, with the secondary entrance on the left. (A6)

Two views of the main foyer, part of which is glazed allowing for a natural lighting which creates a clear and diaphanous atmosphere. A long corridor crosses the first floor to the west side entrance and a stairway leads up to another passageway which runs across the floor above. (B1)

Different perspectives of the corridor which links the different rooms on the upper floor of the building. (7, 8)

THE CENTRE
FOR INTERIOR
DESIGNERS

Bill Bennette & John Solomon

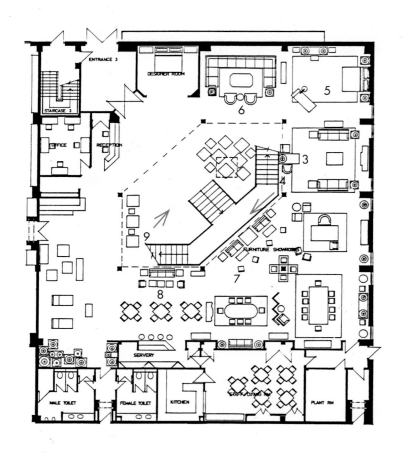

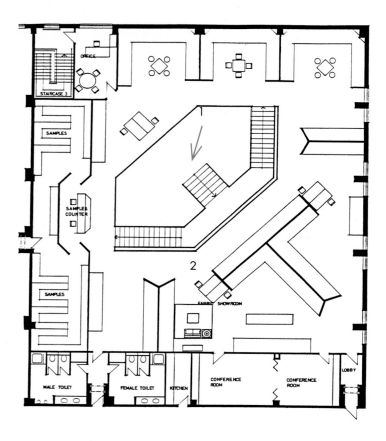

Floor plans of the two floors which make up the premises, with the layout of the different spaces and levels.

On the page opposite, a perspective of the premises illustrating the building's three levels: the entrance, with the stairway that leads down to the basement level, and another which leads up to the second floor. (1)

This centre, the first in Europe created exclusively for designers, interior decorators, architects and professionals who work in the layout and equipment of the interiors of buildings, is similar to other centres which serve the needs of the construction industry. The initiative originated with Charles Hammond, the executive chairman of the company which bears his name, and which was founded in London in 1907.

The design of the project was the work of Bennette and Solomon, two architects who habitually collaborate with this company. Bennette is a specialist in antique furniture, experience which he gained while working with the Victoria and Albert Museum, and whose career had brought him into close con-

tact with the most important professional design associations of Great Britain and the United States, before founding his own design studio in 1972. Solomon has been responsible for a number of outstanding projects in the City and London's West End, where he has been responsible for the design work for the decoration of bank offices and the headquarters of various important companies, as well as the interior design for residential blocks. He has combined his creative work with teaching at the KLC Design School in London.

The centre is based on an easily extendable surface area of close to 1,500 m², which occupies two levels and is linked by a great central stairway. A space, which is eminently

A view of one of the areas of the ground floor, with a variety of furniture articles on display. (2)

suitable for the whole range of styles and colours, was created by conceding an important role to natural lighting, and by choosing a simple and elegant decoration replete with subtle classical reminiscences. Light shades of colour are predominant, both for the walls and the wooden flooring, with the exception of certain details in black and dark brown.

The furniture is exhibited on the ground floor, on the basis of the creation of different groups and ambiences with distinctive personalities. The upper area in great part has been reserved for the exhibition of fabrics, offering more than 4,000 samples hung at a height of 2 metres.

The centre has also been conceived as a workplace, to which professionals from the

On this page, different views of the top floor of the premises, with the display of groups of furniture: a living room (3), a perspective of the area for the display of fabrics and curtains (4) and a display bedroom (5).

On the following page, a living rooms display, on the top floor, in which different ambiences of marked personality and elegance have been created for all kinds of furniture. (6)

Above, an exhibition of a living-dining room (7) and, below, the bar with an area of tables and its own source of lighting, which differentiate it from the other environments created on the second floor. (8)

A perspective of the ground floor and the central stairway. (9)

world of design can go with their clients in order to study the details of their projects, to this end accommodating corners can be found on both floors which are integrated into the space as a whole and yet allow for a certain intimacy. The fundamental idea of these premises is a perfect response to the motto of the Charles Hammond company Quod petit hic est (You will find what you are looking for here).

An office of great classical elegance, with the furniture manufactured using materials of the finest quality and of a traditional design.

WISSENSCHAFTS-
ZENTRUM

James Stirling & Michael Wilford

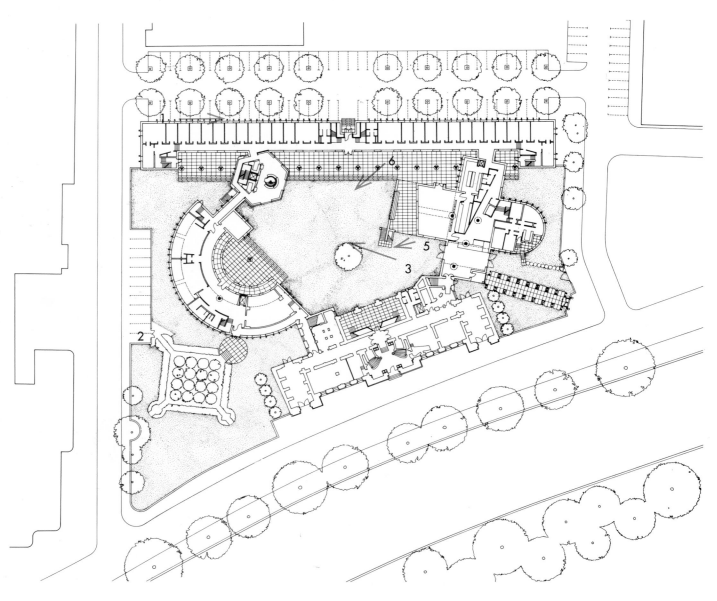

Floor plan of the office complex with the different modules laid out around a large central court.

On the page opposite, above, a perspective of one of the façades illustrating the unusually cheerful and colourful chromatic treatment (1) and, below, a view of the circular building the structure of which is characteristic of the complex as a whole. (2

The architects of this project, realised in Berlin, which takes its inspiration from the monumental presence of an old pre-second world war building and a physically expressive landscape of great typological interest, offer a heterogenous work which seeks to escape the bureaucratic and monotonous air of the classical office complex through the employment of a style which is both vital and dynamic. The articulation of the different bodies around a large central court, and the cheerful and colourful chromatic treatment are the fundamental qualities on which the construction of this Scientific Centre were based.

James Stirling, a Scotsman, graduated from the School of Architecture of the University of Liverpool, and began his professional career working independently until he became associated with James Gowan, in 1956, a collaboration which lasted until 1963. His teaching work has included conferences in the most important British schools and institutions as well as in universities such as Yale. Since 1971 he has been a professor at the Düsseldorf Kunstadekemie, and is an honourary member of many different centres such as the American Institute of Architects, the Florence Academy of Arts and the University of Glasgow. His many awards include the Brunner in 1976, the RIBA Gold Medal in 1980, the Chicago Architecture Award in 1985, and the Praemium Imperiale Award in 1990.

Michael James Wilford, studied at the Kingston Technical School and at the Northern Polytechnic School of Architecture in London. In 1960 he started to work with James Stirling, entering into association with him in 1971. His teaching experience includes presenting papers at conferences in the most prestigious British, American, Canadian and Australian universities and he has also become an honourary member of numerous centres and a judge of the most

71

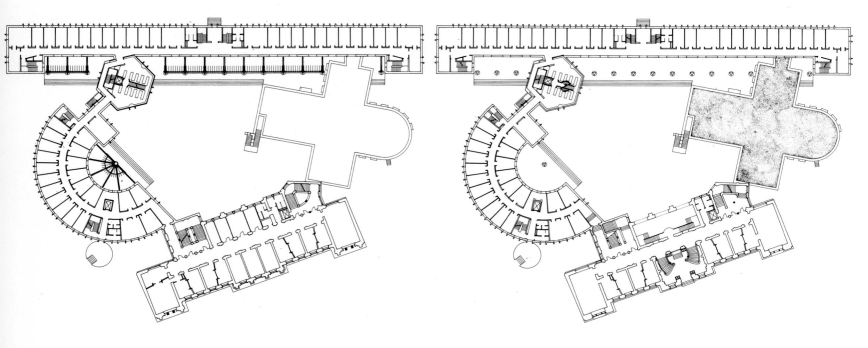

prestigious competitions. His work was recognised with the award of the Hugo Haring Prize, in 1988.

The site is located in an area of urban recuperation, the Berlin Kulturforum, close to the Nationalgalerie of Mies van der Rohe and the office blocks of the Shell Oil Company. The new project would have to make use of the majestic façade of a structure which survived the war, the old School of Fine Arts, and the future complex would have to take advantage of the layout of the building to articulate its new constructive modules so as to be able to confront a widely varied programme of uses.

The creation of a structure capable of housing this group of utilities was the main requirement when it came to the planning of the project. The architects opted for a tactic of continual spatial enclosure, creating a public interior space around which the new modules would be laid out. The overall design pays particular attention to the achievement of the right working atmosphere, through its chromatic treatment, the court and the disconnection, and plurality, of the formal components.

The initial programme included the layout of three separate departments, with a great

On the previous page, a panoramic view of the large central court, with the different constructive modules laid out around it. The plurality of volumes marks out this irregular interior space, with a multiplicity of possible perceptions, and with a great deal of work invested in the public and communication aspects of the different buildings. (3)

Above, floor plans of the two first levels of the complex.

On the page opposite, a perspective of the court, at the foot of the five story semi-cylindrical building, with the column which supports the metallic structure which visually dominates this space. (4)

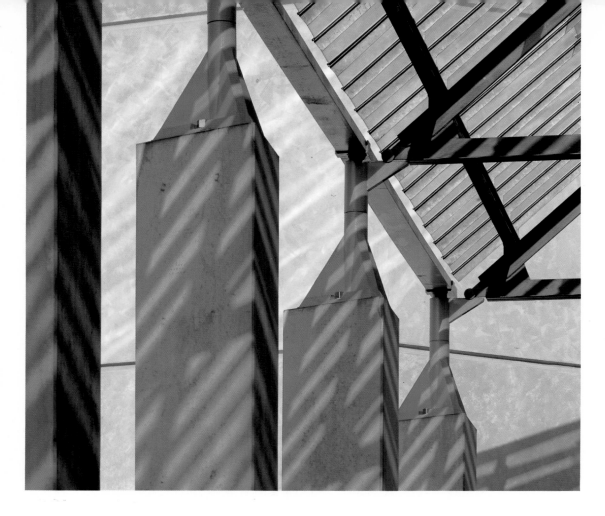

many unicellular offices, an archive library, and also the provision for future extensions. The organisation of these modules around the original building, the interrelation between each module and their reference to the urban landscape, were the principal problems to be dealt with by the proposal for the formal design. These problems were resolved by the application of unifying criteria which related the different buildings to the idea of the court and the enclosing strategy.

The most important constructive modules are the four blocks, which are independent both in terms of volume and function, yet which are specifically organised in a physical relationship in which the interior garden is the fundamental nucleus. This constructive nucleus has acquired a formalisation which is distinct in each case, giving evidence of their individual functions. The five story semi-cylindrical module, for example, connected to a hexagonal tower eight stories high serves as one of the lateral delimiters of the court.

The colourful design of the modules and the strategic layout of the openings has a striking effect. The intention of offering a

Above a detail of the upper part of the columns which support the glazed roof, located above one of the arcades which border the court.

On the page opposite, above, a view of the interior space behind the semi-cylindrical building. The colourful design of the different modules and ornamental details is outstanding, based on a combination of soft blue-toned and rose-coloured sections, which create a warm and welcoming atmosphere. (5) Below, another perspective of the interior court, with the semi-cylindrical building in the background, seen from one of the arcades. (6)

warm and welcoming atmosphere has been achieved through the use of painted stucco, in a structured combination of soft blue toned and rose-coloured sections. A highly dynamic visual rhythm has been achieved through the disposition of the windows, further accentuated by the use of surrounds in the majority of the openings.

The perfectly established functional layout of the different modules, in which the old structure houses the secretariat, the library is located in the vertical tower, and 205 offices are distributed between the remaining modules, according to the departments to which they belong.

On the two previous pages, two views of the main arcade, with the glazed roofing supported by columns of a refined design.

On this page, different views of the previously mentioned arcade, and of one of the wooden structures which roof part of the corridors. On the following page, details of the interior of the building which houses the Scharoun Library.

THE HOLDER GROUP
CENTRAL OFFICE

Isabelle Poulain

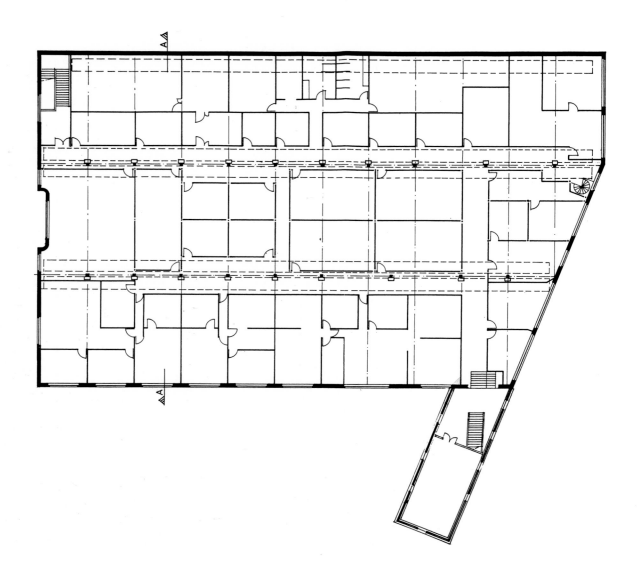

Floor plan of the building with the layout of the different
spaces set aside for the factory itself, the training school
and the company headquarters.

Part of the top floor of the premises, with the stairway in the foreground and a meetings room in the background, illustrating the marked contrast of the building's original brickwork and the new contemporary elements which have been incorporated.

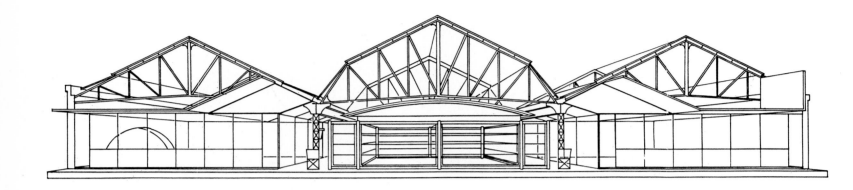

The premises, in Lille, occupied by the head offices of the Holder group of companies, working in the bakery sector with over a hundred establishments in France (as well as branches in Texas and Louisiana), had become too small for their expanding organisation and the chairman of the group, Francis Holder, decided to acquire an enormous old abandoned building in the industrial area of the city. This old warehouse of proven solidity needed a thorough refurbishment in order to hold the new company headquarters, the interior had to be completely transformed, maintaining only the image of strength and security transmitted by the exterior of the building.

Isabelle Poulain, the project architect, is a graduate in architecture and fine arts, and a working professional of recognised prestige at the head of her own practice in Paris, which she founded in 1984. Her professional work, which she has combined with teaching in a school in the French capital where she runs a course on Materials and Methods, has included a series of interesting projects, principally commercial spaces, offices and restaurants. Fine examples of the above are various fashion shops in Paris, the offices of several

advertising agencies and restaurants such as Bwana Jones, in Lille. Her work has also been publicised in prestigious specialist magazines.

The space of the old building would have to house an industrial freezing line, a training school and the offices themselves, with their meetings rooms and directors suites. The aim was to create an authentic complex within the red brick walls, which would be diverse, functional and practical. The decoration is based on a response to this idea, adopting such bold solutions as the full visibility of the complete system of air-conditioning and the various technical connections.

Poulain has achieved the design of a space which, without discounting purely aesthetic considerations, has been converted into an absolutely functional and practical centre.

An elevation section of the building, marking a clear distinction between the three modules.

An interior view of the first floor, with one of the newly created areas, characterised by the predominance of metallic structures and the glazed surfaces of the walls and the ceilings.

A view of one of the office areas on the top floor, the glazed wall surfaces allowing the natural light to flood in.

Above, a perspective of one of the offices on the top floor, vividly contrasting the original brickwork wall with the incorporated metallic structures and the glazing.

Below, a view of the ground floor of the premises, illustrating the clearly mechanistic aesthetics.

UFFICI MICROFIN

Epton Studio

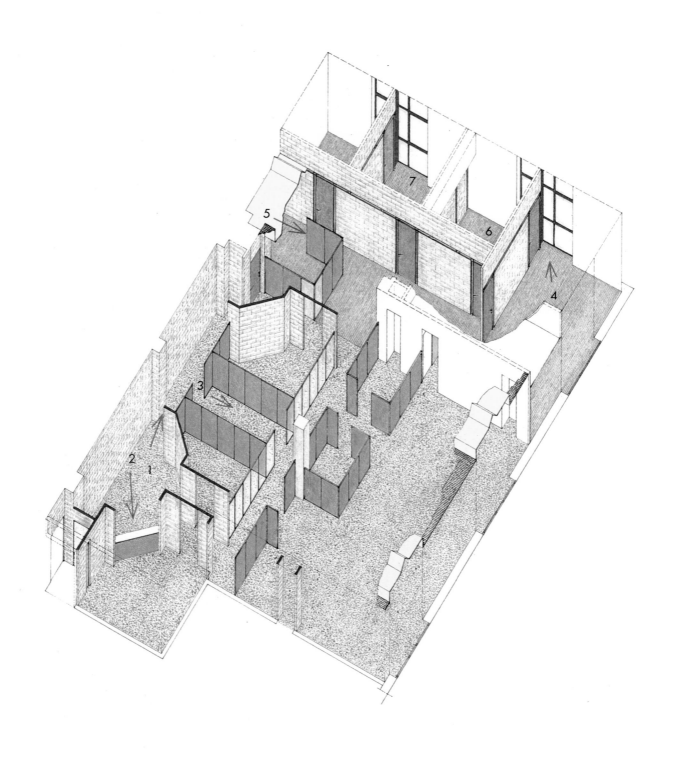

The head office of the Microfin company is located on the third floor of a building in Turin which dates from the turn of the century. The company works in software and telematic, automotive and transport subsystems, providing quality products for a prestigious clientele in a mainly professional field.

Epton Studio was founded in 1982, in Turin, the native city of its three founder members, Emmanuela Barberini, Marina Gariboldi and Guilia Sarti. The professional experience of these three architects includes investigation projects (for CNR and CIEPA) and town planning projects in Albissola, Mare and Pescara. They have worked on projects for public buildings in Turin, including the rebuilding of the Palazzo a Vela, the new headquarters of the Data Elaboration Service of the Polytechnic of Turin and the Stadio Comunale. Their professional careers, however, have been focused on the refurbishing and design of commercial and residential spaces, such as Cristal Art, the Vicenza Galleries and the Juvarra Theatre.

The Microfin offices occupy a vast space, 900 m², with an open plan floor only interrupted by pilasters and the openings set aside

On the page opposite, floor plan showing the layout of the different functional spaces of the Microfin company headquarters.

On this page, a view of one of the communicating areas. The exposed Leca brickwork walls stop short of the ceil-

for the housing of the electrical installations. The walls have a height of 4.70 m, which further exaggerates the perception of the space. The spaces required by the company included: a reception area, an open space for the future installation of eight work posts for the computer programmers, a series of isolated offices (which were established through a system of moveable walls), the directors suites and, finally, the washrooms.

The 2.7 m high exposed brick walls stop short of the ceiling, the aim of which is to encourage the perception of continuity and to allow for the limited light that filters through from the one, and only, external wall to permeate the whole of the premises. These walls contribute to the more precise definition of the space set aside for the offices, the meetings room and the reception area.

From a formal point of view the aesthetic options chosen by the three architects found their inspiration in the typically industrial characteristics of the building, as well as responding to the functional needs of the company, with regard to the establishing of an elegant and sophisticated image. The grey block walls offer ample evidences of this, evoking the particular typology of this kind of structure.

Apart from the walls, mentioned above, the materials used are of great interest; the flooring installed in the premises as a whole is Vieropierre, consisting of small grains of flint set with synthetic resin and coloured by chemical processing. In order to establish a certain visual hierarchy the flooring in the management area is of parquet, identified with the idea of comfort.

The distinct categories of the different areas are also expressed by means of the low level ceilings, with wooden gratings and coal grey aluminium tiles in the offices of the programmers, while the option of plaster panels mounted with stucco jointing was chosen for the management area.

The furniture and the decorative elements confer an air of finely judged balance between easy going comfort and functional austerity, throughout the premises, in combinations which succeed in creating the most suitable of working environments. The office of the Chairman presents a collection of the most prestigious design names: the fine quality desk from the Burdik Group, the Soft Pad seating, the bookshelves by Dieter Rams and the Velo lamps created by Ingo Maurer for Fontana Arte. The directors offices are decorated with a sombre table by New Bird, with Aluminium Group seating which grants them

A view of the extended entrance and reception area. Grains of flint, set with synthetic resin and with the colour added by synthetic means have been used for the flooring of the communal areas; the result is sober and at the same time elegant. (2)

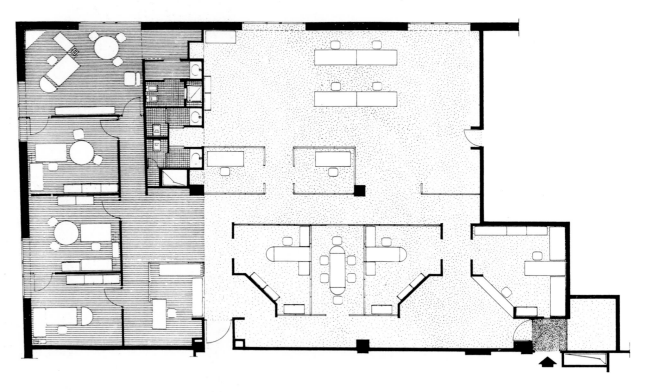

Above, floor plan of the premises, with the layout of the
different spaces.

Below, and on the page opposite, views of one of the corridors and the meetings room. (3)

a serious yet attractive atmosphere. The open plan space and the work rooms are equipped with New Bird desks and Supporto chairs. The reception area boasts one of the most audacious pieces, the Cannaregio sofa, by the Italian company Cassina, which adds a splash of colour to premises which are otherwise decidedly discreet.

These three Italian designers and architects have realised, through the creation and the distribution of the space, its design and interior decoration, an outstandingly talented exercise in the creation of a neutral and functional work centre which is entirely suited to the needs of the company. However, with an indispensable input of their highly personalised sense of design they have managed to instill the space with its own brilliant and unique identity.

Above, a view of one of the offices in the management area. Here the flooring is parquet, establishing a hierarchical differentiation, and conferring a sensation of greater comfort. (4)

On the page opposite, one of the communicating passageways, with the programmers offices on the right. (5)

A perspective of one of the corridors.

On the page opposite, two of the executive offices. Through the furniture and the decorative elements an atmosphere balanced between a certain sense of comfort and a functional austerity is granted to the different areas. (6,7)

MINISTRY OF FOREIGN AFFAIRS- THE HAGUE

Ruud Bartijn & Theo Tempelman

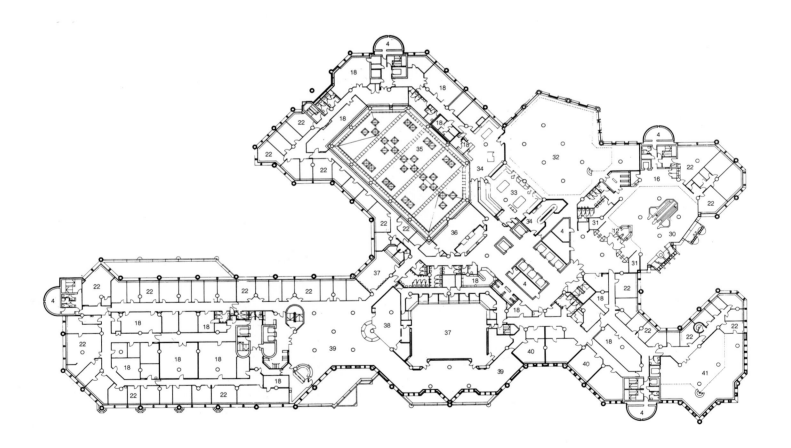

Floor plan of the first level of the building.

Above, a view of the press centre from the upper tribune.

Below, the conference hall of the Ministry of Foreign Affairs.

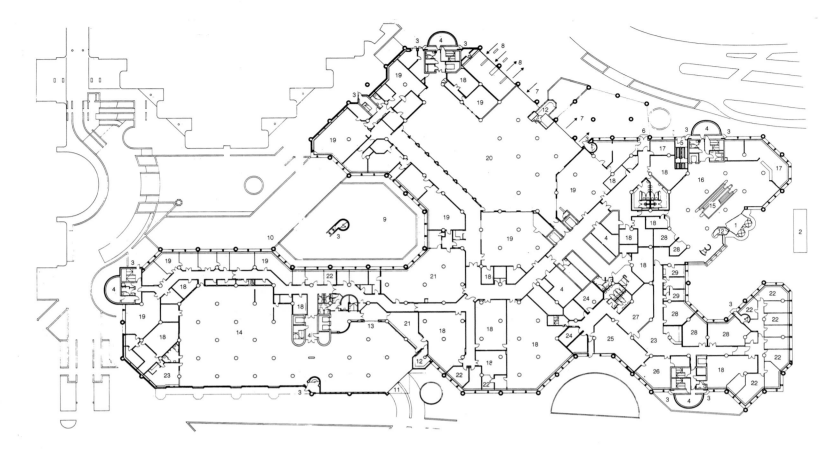

A floor plan of the second floor of the building.

The architect D.C. Apon who originated the project for the Ministry of Foreign Affairs building in the Hague, decided to highlight the interior structure in relation to the exterior through the unification of the materials used: concrete, grey and brown brickwork and dark brown aluminium. The interior design was created by the Salomonson, Tempelman & Egberts (STE) architectural practice, with Theo Tempelman and Ruud Bartijn directing the work.

Ruud Bartijn graduated in architecture from the Technical University of Eindhoven in 1976, and in 1978 he began his association with Architecten Associatie STE, becoming a partner five years later. He has been responsible for projects for dwellings, offices, clinics and for a variety of interior design work. Tempelman was born in Indonesia and moved to Holland after the war. He studied interior design at the Academie voor Bouwkunst en Industrie and was a lecturer at the Academie van Beeldende Kunst, in the Hague, between 1970 and 1975. In 1974 he founded the

A view of the conference hall, with the translation booths in the background. The design of the lighting system, based on halogen spots and a spectacular central lighting structure suspended from steel cables is of great interest.

Architecten Asociatie STE practice in Amsterdam and Arnhem, together with Salomonson and Egberts, designing furniture for offices, restaurants, libraries and public buildings.

The outstanding spaces of the Ministry of Foreign Affairs are the Conference hall, the press centre and the staff working areas, all of which manage to transmit an international atmosphere partly achieved through the materials employed and the treatment which they have been given. The most evident material is ash wood, for the ceilings, walls and doors; for the furniture in general; and in the conference hall, this material also performs an important acoustic function. The lighting in the conference hall was specially designed

Above, the foyer of the conference hall, with its unusual
sloping ceiling, in wood and partly glazed.

Below, another perspective of the press centre.

suspended from steel cables and occupies the very centre of the space.

In the press centre a finely judged harmony has been achieved between the different materials used for the lighting and the technical and acoustic installations.

On the second floor there is a library, also predominantly in ash wood, where the walls are clad with plastic panels reflecting the same brown tone used on the exterior of the building. The decoration of the staff restaurant is again based on ash wood with the inclusion of the necessary conditioning, in the upper part, to dull the noise of the dining area.

In summary, the interior of the Ministry of Foreign Affairs is, at the present time, a multifunctional space in which a sober elegance creates an atmosphere which is suitable for work, and fosters interpersonal relationships.

A view of a corner of the library, with the circular metal stairway connecting the different levels.

An exterior view of the building which houses the headquarters of the Dutch Ministry of Foreign Affairs.

Different details of the passageway and corridors.

Above, a view of the staff dining room and, below, the foyer of the conference hall.

THE CHIAT/DAY
ADVERTISING
OFFICES

Stefano de Martino

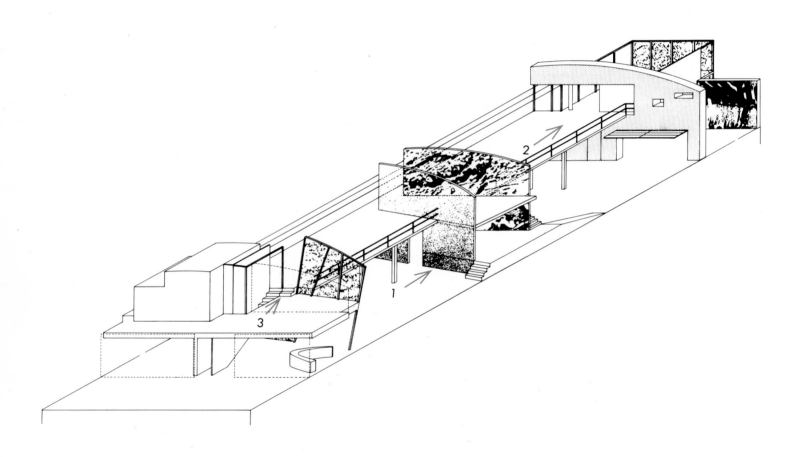

Elevation section of the Chiat/Day agency offices in London. (A)

On the page opposite, a view of one of the communicating areas of the lower floor. At the end one of the translucent glass fibre screens which are a constant feature of the decoration of the premises. (A1)

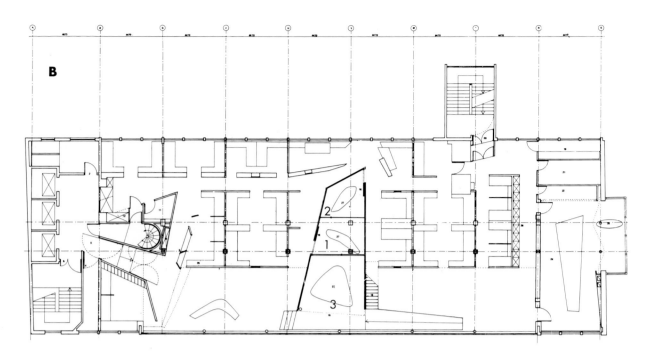

B

Floor plans of the premises, with the lower level (above)
and, below, the double height top floor added later and
roofed with a glazed vaulted structure. (B,C)

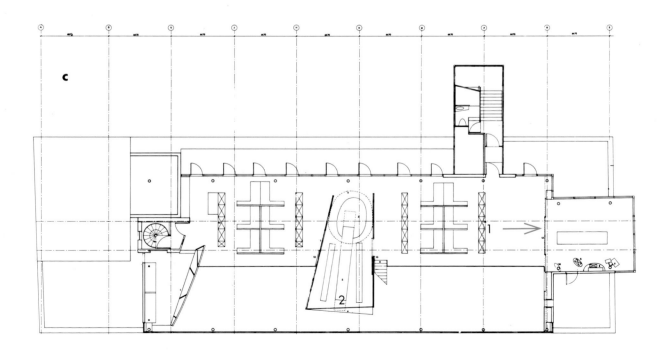

C

The interior of the London headquarters of the Chiat/Day advertising agency was designed by the Italian architect, Stefano de Martino, who with this project has achieved one of the most attractive and interesting interiors of recent years, his principal message being conveyed by the contrast between architectural rigor and asymmetrical design. Many of the most brilliant aspects of the interior design of the workplace are concentrated on the two levels of this building, including the creation of autonomous and differentiated spaces in an attempt to give a more human face to the monotony of the working environment and to establish a visual connection with the exterior, with the glazed area of the top floor offering a panoramic view of the surrounding area.

Stefano de Martino graduated in architecture at the Bartlett School of Architecture in 1977, and was awarded an Honourary Diploma by the Architectural Association in

Different views of the furniture, with various of the pieces, excepting the office chairs, designed by Stefano Martino himself.

One of the work rooms for the creative staff of the agency.

1979. This same year he joined the Office for Metropolitan Architecture (OMA), a collaboration which lasted until 1983. During these years he participated in numerous projects and competitions, including: the Parc de la Villette in Paris, the Netherlands Dance Theatre, and a bridge and apartment buildings in Rotterdam. Between 1983 and 1989 he worked in association with Alex Wall,

combining research with teaching in the Architectural Association and project work. Proposals for the Ace Cinema in Brixton, the Royal Docks and Beckton, the Docklands Museum and Le Murate in Florence. From that period in his career the Artists House in Holland Park and the Cities of Childhood exhibition, which was shown throughout Europe, are worthy of special mention. In

A perspective of the room for meetings and the presentation of new advertising campaigns, the glass walls offering a spectacular panoramic view of the city. (A2), (C1)

Communicating stairway between the different levels (A3) and, below, one of the small meeting rooms.

1989 he founded his own practice in London and in the first year developed a plan for an aquatic sports centre in the Isle of Wight. The most interesting of his recent projects include a villa for the Architectural Festival in the Hague.

The building, in which the Chiat/Day agency offices are located, is a modest town house built in the seventies and redesigned by the DEGW team. The principal addition is a double-height top floor built as an extension to the existing roof and with a new vaulted and glazed structure. It was this space which the advertising agency chose for its European headquarters.

The premises are divided into two easily intercommunicated levels and, in this sense, the translucent glass panels play an important role as an ideal means of distribution, due to their versatility and their capacity to project the natural light. This uncomplicated system allows for the creation of independent work areas that remain in visual contact with the rest of the space. This strategy serves to confirm the expressed intention to organise the space in a heterogenous manner, renouncing a rigid compartmentalisation and, at the same time, granting each of these areas its own personality. There are no corridors, in the conventional sense, nor a lineal sequence of rooms, and yet each of the spaces has been resolved with the aim of fulfilling its specific functional needs.

Through this dynamic system of distribution, the three essential areas are laid out on the two levels which house the different modules and rooms. The first includes the large

A detail of one of the communicating areas. The design of the interior space is characterised by the unusual chromatic treatment, and also by the capricious forms which combine curves and straight lines.

One of the meeting rooms characterised by its irregular design, its autonomy and the unusual design of the furniture. These characteristics are a constant throughout the small meeting rooms. (A2)

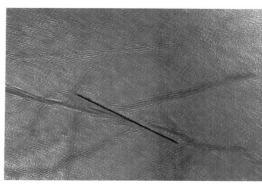

Another of the meeting rooms of a different design from
the last, and with a table of a different colour. (A1)

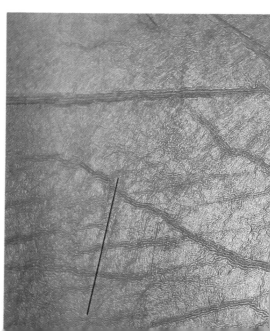

113

A perspective of the extension of the upper floor, consisting of a platform which houses a meetings area, dominated by a large wooden table and benches of an original design. (C2)

screen at the entrance, which separates the foyer from the offices, at the same time as it creates secondary production spaces, the dark room, the fire escape, and a platform which houses the audio-visual library.

The intermediate area constitutes the central nucleus of the premises, laid out at a double height between two glazed surfaces, and elevated with respect to the general level. Various meeting rooms of an irregular design are located here, alongside storage sections and the extension of the upper floor in the form of a second platform, shaped like a cradle, which projects out beyond the first.

Access to the top floor is gained by a staircase with a weightless feel which backs onto one of the glass surfaces. The last area corre-

A third meeting room located in the middle area of the premises. (B3)

sponds to this built-on structure realised by DEGW. The main conference room is housed on the lower floor, along with secondary installations, while the top floor houses a meetings space.

All of the furniture was designed by Martino, with the assistance of a team of specialists. The chromatic treatment is a very important component of the interior aesthetic treatment, as is the predominance of voluptuous biomorphic curved forms.

OFFICES OF A SERVICE COMPANY

Wortmann Bañares Arquitectos

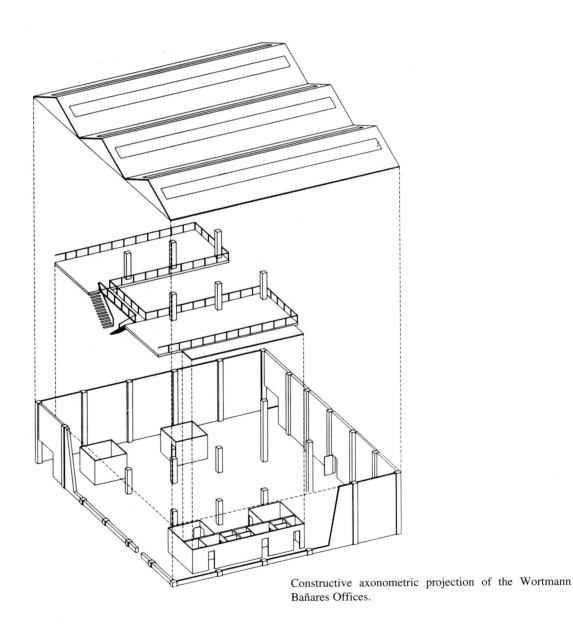

Constructive axonometric projection of the Wortmann Bañares Offices.

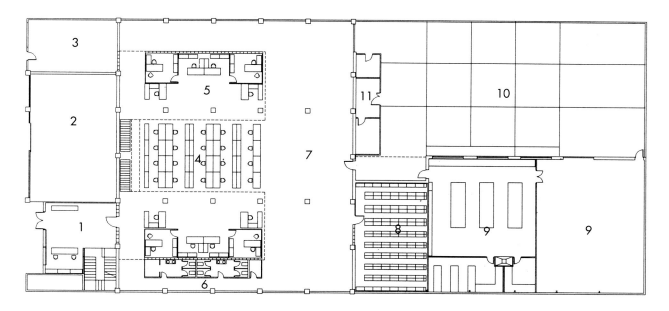

Above, floor plan and distribution plan of the ground floor
of the premises.

1. Main entrance and reception area
2. Garage
3. Truck entrance
4. Inspector's area
5. Inspection management
6. Washrooms
7. Growth space
8. Archive
9. Laboratory
10. Courtyard
11. Installations

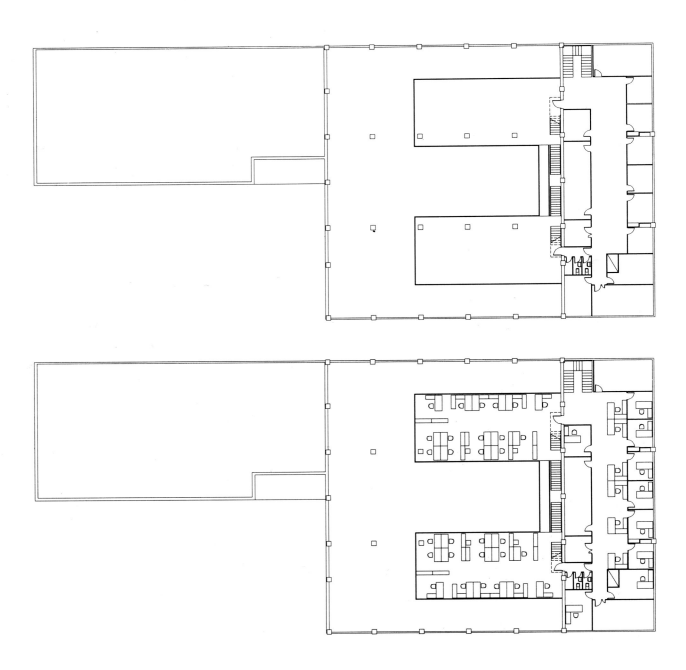

Floor plan and plan distribution of the mezzanine level.

On the page opposite, a view of the long work tables in the central area between the two mezzanine levels.

A perspective of the walkway between the two mezzanine levels.

The adaptation of an industrial plant, on the outskirts of Barcelona, for the headquarters of a service company gave rise to a project which combined great quality both in terms of space and of the work site, with a cost far below that of a conventional office building.

The project went ahead on the basis of fulfilling, in so far as it was possible, the economic objectives marked out by the client. This objective was achieved thanks to a suitable design and exhaustive project planning.

The integral realisation of this project was entrusted to Wortmann Bañares Architects, WB, S.A.. The Practice evolved from the collaboration between the architects Guillermo Bañares and Johannes Kaiser Wortmann who have, for the last ten years, been working on projects, consultations and the control of important architectural sites. One of the basic characteristics of the work of the practice is the ensuring of a precise and effective development of the planning process, and the execution of the work itself. This Spanish-German team have taken on the role of a bridge, uniting the conceptual and procedural differences between Spain and Germany. WB, S.A. has also been a member of the German Chamber of Commerce since 1991.

The architects claim that the particular challenge of this project was the preservation of the extensive and well lit space of the industrial plant, while creating attractive and comfortable working conditions. The immense height of the premises, which proved problematic in so far as its use as office space, was turned into an advantage through the installation of an extensive mezzanine level. The open plan work posts, which did not require compartmentalising, were located on this level. Below the mezzanine level, which also serves to communicate the installations, there are four individual offices with dependant areas for secretaries, etc., and the washrooms. The centre of the floor is occupied by

Another view of the long work tables in the central work area.

long work tables for the use of the inspectors, who do not need individual office space, spending the greater part of their working day out of the office.

The architects interpreted the scarcity of the available budget as an incentive to apply solutions based on prefabricated industrial elements, exploiting the relatively low cost, and the aesthetics of this unusual utilitarian architectural style. A special design for the work tables was also developed by the architects, along these same lines.

Encouraged by the great success achieved by these measures the client is planning to apply the new image to the rest of his offices in a progressive manager.

The central area, a space with a double height.

On the previous page, open plan work post in the inspection management sector.

A view of the inspector's area.

MULTIPURPOSE HALL FOR THE SOCIEDAD NESTLÉ

Ll. Pau, J. Martorell, O. Bohigas & D. Mackay

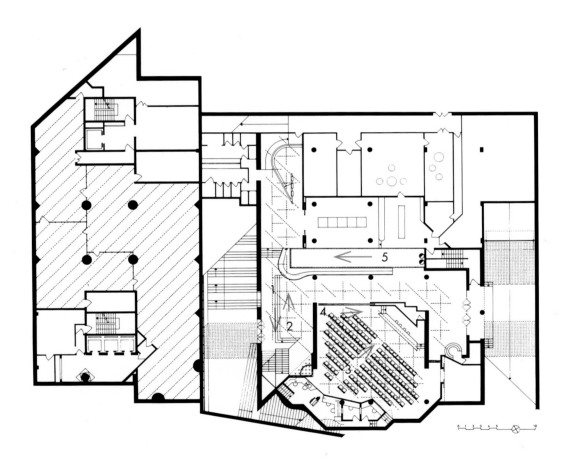

Floor plan of the multipurpose hall in the Nestlé office complex, with the layout of the different areas

Iron stairway, which leads to the upper level of the premises. (1)

Below, a perspective of one of the communication areas, with two of the accesses, steps and a ramp with a gentle slope. (2)

Details of the stairways which connect the different levels of the premises, in a blue tone, vividly contrasting with the red of the curtains.

A partial view of the conference room. (3)

The new office building for the Sociedad Nestlé in Esplugues, Barcelona, in reality is an extension of the neighbouring complex built in the nineteen seventies. The project was taken on by a prestigious group of architects, Lluís Pau, Josep Martorell, Oriol Bohigas and David Mackay. In 1973 Pau joined the practice of the other three architects, where he took charge of the IDP, working on interior design and the mounting of exhibitions. Together they have worked on many projects including: the design for the libraries network for the Generalitat of Catalonia, the new image of the Seat/Volkswagen/Audi salerooms, the offices of the Caixa de Catalunya, The Association of Attorneys and various cultural centres, shops and hotels.

A tunnel bridge crosses over the garden linking the two office buildings, and also serving as the access to the first level of the basement by way of a steel and glass stairway. The multipurpose hallway is located on this level, which, together with the ground floor foyers is a space set aside for the diffusion of information to visitors and clients.

Perspectives of the conference room, from a different angle. (4)

Because of its intermediate position between the buildings, this floor consists of two large functional areas, separated by a court infiltrated by the natural light from the garden. The first area, on a lower level, consists of a functions room, with a moveable tribune, a centre for simultaneous translation, storage space and control rooms for the audiovisual equipment. There is also an area set aside for receptions with a bar/office.

The second area, on an upper level, houses the kitchen, the tasting and demonstration rooms, and a cloakroom and washrooms. The containing walls are clad with horizontal bands, alternating polished sandstone, and white formica, with wooden panels and red curtains separating the hall from the foyers as and when required to do so. The flooring is covered with hardwearing carpet in the foyers, and in the other spaces with a uniform flooring of intense green terrazzo.

This Hall for the Sociedad Nestlé is, then, a multipurpose area where the architects have combined an absolute functionality with the most avant-garde design.

A view of the access ramp to the upper level, where there are service areas, such as the kitchen the tasting room and the cloakroom. (5)

SERNIT

Claude Vasconi

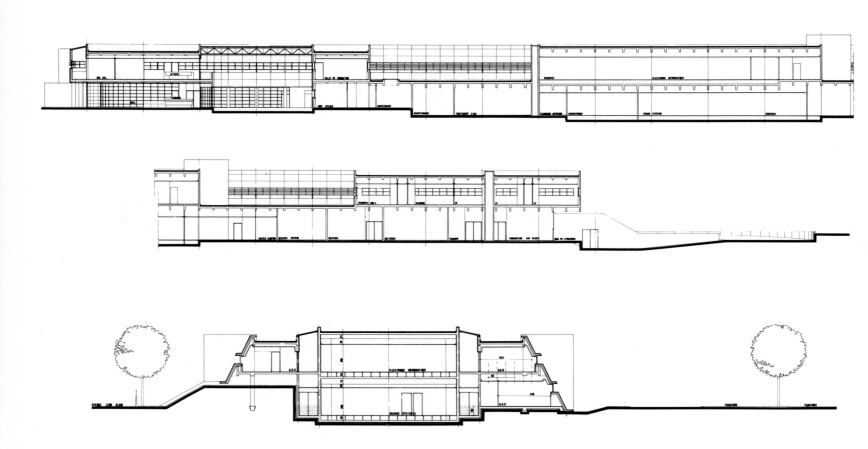

Elevation sections of the three modules which make up the building; the two lateral volumes and the central body.

On the page opposite, a view of the internal court located in the reception area, illustrating the curved forms in contrast to the rigidity which predominates in the rest of the complex. The system of glazing and the rhythmic disposition of the pillars, together with the presence of a small garden area, suggest a welcoming atmosphere, contrasted with the technological coldness of the aesthetic of the building as a whole. (1)

In 1990 the construction work was finished on this communications technical research centre, the Logical Engineering Research and Development Unit in Grenoble. The developer had clearly stated the objectives: architectural quality, technical solutions replete with aesthetic values and a balanced relation between the price and the result. The projection of a unitary construction with a monolithic aspect which would be an expression of values such as control, protection and independence was required. The internal layout would also have to present itself in a way that was clearly dissociated from, with an evident distancing from the laboratory area, the administrative area and those spaces set aside for calculation and technical work. On this basis the pro-

ject was entrusted to Claude Vasconi, presenting him with a new challenge to his tried and tested strategy of combining technology and architecture.

Claude Vasconi graduated in 1964 from the National School of Arts and Industry in Strasbourg. In 1969 he founded his own practice, working on large scale installations in the area of Cergy-Pontoise, Intertional Police Station in Val d'Oise and the Trois Fontaines Commercial Centre. Between 1973 and 1979 he was responsible for such important projects as the Forum de Halles and the Cergy-Pontoise Cultural Centre, as well as various public housing projects in municipal districts around Paris. In 1979 his work was recognised with the award of French architecture's Grand Prix. During the eighties he

On the previous page, a perspective of part of the central module. Above one of the lateral modules which make up the building. (2)

worked on many projects including: the Tour Hertziana in Romainville, for TDF; the Saint Germain-en-Laye National Police Station; the Coeur de Ville de Saint Nazaire; a university residence in Strasbourg; the Thomson Factory in Valenciennes; the Hotel du Departement in Bas-Rhin, also in Strasbourg; the Ministry of the Economy; and the Opera of the Bastille. Among his most recent projects special mention should be made of the Palace of Congresses and the Opera of Montpelier, the Ville de Vitrolles centre, the Information Technology Building of the General Treasury in Marseilles, the National Print Works in Bondoufle, the Lille World Trade Centre and the Congress Centre in Reims.

The project for the Sernit complex had to be based on an architectural language which would make the functional contents visible from the exterior. In order to achieve this objective Vasconi concentrated the technical spaces and the calculations centre (the main components par excellence) in a central module. In order to ensure the maximum level of protection, an artificial semi-elevation was erected, half burying these spaces, and around which the two lineal modules, that would complete the complex, were distributed.

These two lengthways module house the research laboratories with the exterior

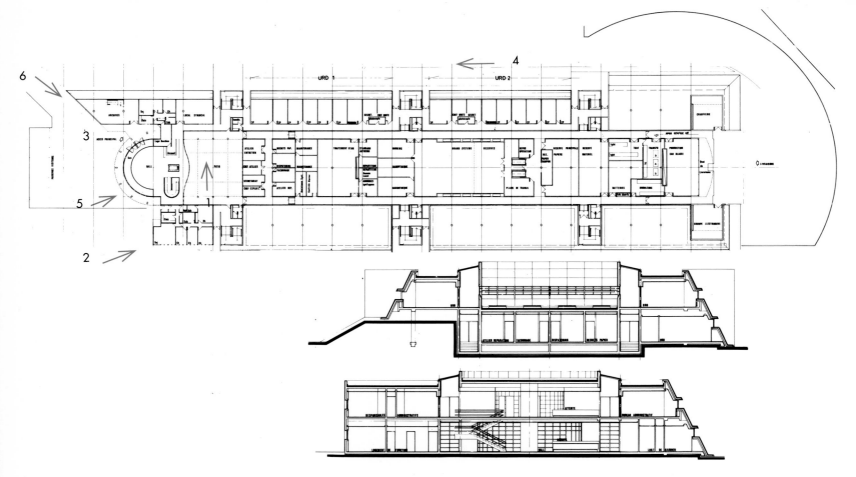

façades presenting an intriguing inclination. The administration offices are located between the two flanks of these modules, linked to one of the entrances. For purely functional and organisational reasons some of the service rooms, such as the training rooms and the library, are located in these lateral modules.

Through the application of this architectural hierarchy, based on a differentiation of levels, a system of emplacements serves to visually distribute the different functional contents.

The definitive layout of the centre is based on three essential areas, according to the activities that are carried out in each of them. The intermediate volume is dedicated to work which is of a more public nature, and is therefore situated close to the entrance. Consequently a separate main access was built presenting a less severe image of the building. This, in turn, contrasted with the two lateral modules with their opaque mineral connotations, the gentle semi-circular form of the central module, located on the southern slope extenuates the process of transition towards the interior. A system of glazing was

Floor plan of the building and elevation sections. On the page opposite, above, a view of the main entrance (3) and, below, one of the interior work areas, in the majority of which lengthways glazing has been installed, which from the outside appear to be continuous bands presenting a great visual symmetry.

138

used for this end, together with a rhythmic disposition of pillars which support the emergent volumetric mass.

In the foyer there is a large open space, in the style of an interior court, where receptions and other events are held. This sector appears to be covered over by a glazed wall surface which provides an intense, yet pleasant, natural lighting. A garden area, a lift which communicates the services areas on the upper floors and the sinuous ramp, which runs parallel to the library façade, supported by columns, are the most representative elements of this interior area.

Access to the administrative and management modules is gained laterally, by a private stairway fitted with security control installations. The services areas have been located as close as possible to the offices and research laboratories. The experimental units are shared out among the different lateral buildings and the central module. Both the sector dedicated to information technology and the calculation centre are restricted areas and have been given a special treatment.

This building designed by Vasconi offers an original combination of expressive architecture and pragmatic rigour, even considering the great importance which has been conceded to its purely functional aspects, the architect has still managed to realise a brilliant exercise in style based on the fragmentation of the modules and levels and granting the exteriors an imposing and futuristic aspect whilst maintaining a fluid visual dynamic.

On the two previous pages, above, a perspective of the façade of one of the lateral modules (4) and, below, a view of one of the access areas (5). On this and the following page, another view of the façade, a paradigmatic example of the aesthetic language of the architect, based on innovative and avant-garde criteria. (6)

TIEMPO / BBDO OFFICES

Tonet Sunyer & Jordi Badia

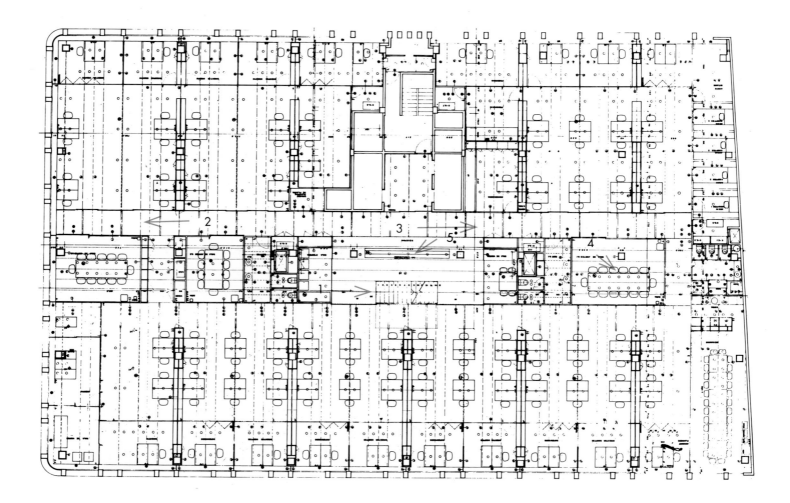

Floor plan of the first level of the offices, the structure of which is repeated on the second floor, illustrating the division into three long sections delimited by corridors, in which the central section serves as the reception and services area, while the other sections are set aside for purely working functions.

The projet by Tonet Sunyer and Jordi Badia for the offices of the Tiempo/BBDO advertising agency in Barcelona was one of the finalists for the FAD Design Prize. The creativity of the design was heavily influenced by the nature of the physical space, and also had to adapt itself to the aesthetic and atmospheric structural limitations of the premises. The original idea was to create an accessible image which would be warm and comfortable, yet absolutely functional.

Tonet Sunyer graduated in architecture from ETSAB, in Barcelona, where he currently works as a lecturer. His work has won him recognition from the FAD Prizes: he was a finalist in the architecture, restoration and interior design categories, in 1983 and 1984; he was awarded the Joaquín Berao Jewellery Prize, also in 1984; in 1986 and 1987 he was a finalist for the Casa Nassia Award, winning it in 1989. Jordi Badia also studied architecture at ETSAB and is currently the projects professor at the Elisava School of Design. He has worked with Tonet Sunyer since 1986, and since 1989 has shared the same studio.

Different perspectives of the offices, above, the metallic stairway located behind the reception counter (1), a part of the administrative area in the central sector, and, below, one of the offices in the creative department.

A selection of the outstanding projects in which they have worked together would have to include the Casa Senón, in Valencia, and the Casa Regina, in Barcelona. Individually their work includes the Archaeological Museum in Tarragona, The Centre for the Protection of Minors in Badalona, an office building for the Granollers Town Hall and the Bar Bijou in Barcelona.

The premises consist of two intercommunicating floors, with the same structural base, a rectangular floor divided into three long sectors. The central sector has a services area and the offices and working spaces are located in the lateral sectors.

The reception area is on the level of the first floor, in the central sector, and is charac-

A perspective of the passage way which runs from the right of the entrance doorway (2) and, beside this, a general view of the reception area. (3)

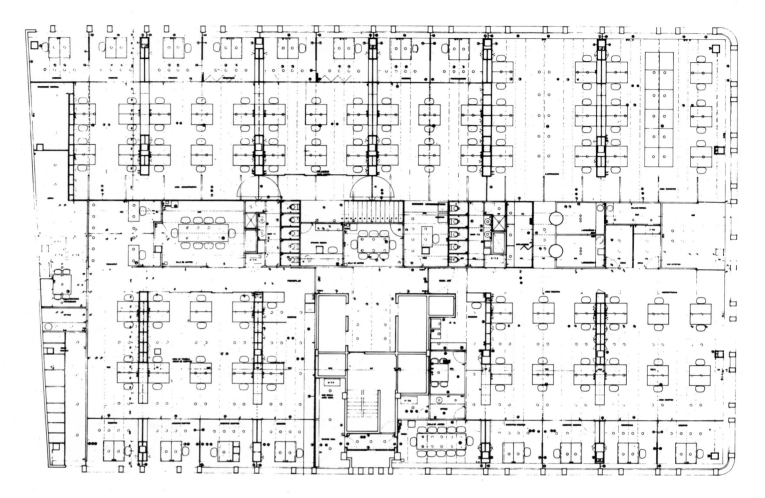

terised by rounded geometric forms which are softened by a pleasant combination of colours and the textures of the materials employed, furnishing the area of the entrance with a warm and welcoming air. To one side there are the meeting rooms and the waiting rooms for the visitors.

The two long lateral spaces, at either side of the central area, share the same completely longitudinal spatial perspective. The offices are located in these areas, separated by two long corridors which run parallel to the central sector.

These spaces are divided by a system of partitions and separators which compartmentalise the offices, facilitating the creation of work groups. The same structural division of the space is repeated on the top floor of the premises.

The interior design, in addition to the creation of a system for the division of space, consists in giving each work area an aesthetic treatment related to its functions. Thus, once the purely structural problems had been resolved, a great variety of strategies were used to define the individual spaces, including the use of different combinations of colours and textures which played a decisive role in the conceptual design of each area.

The colour scheme in general was kept as unintrusive as possible in the work areas, given that their own dynamics and the multiplicity of activities in which the advertising agency is engaged provide the necessary

Floor plan of the second level, with a structure which is practically identical to that of the lower floor.

A view of one of the meeting rooms on the ground floor, decorated in warm tones which contrast with the chromatic coolness of the passage ways. (4)

One of the offices in the creative department.

colour and vitality for each of these spaces. The shades of colour in the central sector are exaggeratedly warm, in a marked contrast to the rest.

The most important design aspects of the project were related to the reception area. The geometric lines are emphasised by the aesthetic interplay of the combination of wood and glass in the reception counter. The textures and colours of the furniture create a pleasant and welcoming atmosphere which is emphasised by the gentle halogen spot lighting. Two elements complete the design of this space, the consciously asymmetrical tinted glass panel, and the metallic stairway which links the two levels of the premises.

The reception area leads to the waiting rooms for the visitors which are designed on the basis of the aesthetic models which are predominant throughout this area. The idea is that the person who enters the agency should experience a welcoming sensation through the warmth of the colours, materials and forms, which are counterpointed by the blue and green tones used for the decoration of the adjacent corridors.

Sunyer and Badia successfully resolved the spatial and structural limitations of the premises with a project which is defined by the creativity of the input and the purity of the design content, combined in an almost perfect synthesis of architectural conceptualisation and creative design.

Part of the offices area, illustrating the lack of classical or partition walls, and the use of low level partitions and elements of the furniture to establish a division of the space.

151

THE DESIGNERS' SOCIETY HEADQUARTERS

Dinah Casson & Roger Mann

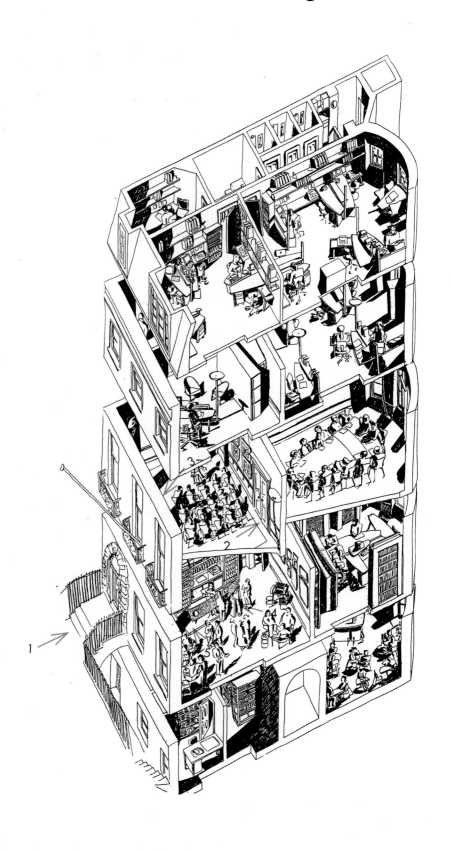

On the page opposite, a plan of the building with the layout of the different sectors and rooms.

A view of the entrance to the Headquarters of the Society, from Bedford Square (1), below, a perspective of the reception area, with the access door in the background and the aluminium counter in the foreground.

The headquarters of the Society of Designers is located in Bedford Square, a London residential square in the Georgian style which now houses various offices. Because of the historical importance of this area the English Heritage Council dictated strict regulations to control any interior or exterior alterations ruling out any reform which did not pay its due respects to the history of the buildings in the area. Before the move, the Society of Designers, a professional association with some 12,000 members, occupied a floor above the Institute of Contemporary Arts, but the desire to create a new defined public image led them to change the location of their headquarters.

The project was placed in the hands of Dinnah Casson and Roger Mann, who have

Part of the wall surface of one of the rooms, with the specially commissioned painted paper including fragments of the Society's magazine.

worked as a team since 1984, although they have also collaborated with other designers and architects on interior design, furniture design and exhibition projects during this time. Mann is a guest lecturer at the Kingston Polytechnic and Casson is the director of the Middlesex Polytechnic and a professor at the Royal College of Art. Their work includes many projects, including the Grangelato ice-cream shops and the offices of The Guardian newspaper. Their more recent work includes the mounting of an exhibition on British Designers, in the Boymans Museum in Rotterdam, and book designs for a prestigious Italian publisher.

For the redesign of the Bedford Square building, the painting of multi-colour figures on the ceilings was suggested to the English Heritage Council who rejected the proposal, as it was felt that this treatment would lower the dignity of the premises and spoil the historical character which they were attempting to preserve.

The entrance is a typical foyer, leading directly to the stairs and to the two rooms on the ground floor. The reception counter is made of aluminium and reflects the white and

A perspective of one of the meeting rooms. (2)

On this page, two of the rooms used for parties and meetings.

A view of one of the meeting rooms, with the wooden floor boards which are common to all of the rooms. (3)

black floor tiles. With the bar an effort was made to avoid any resemblance to a typical bar through the use of a long recess with suspended projections for tables. In the library the typical built in shelving was rejected in favour of bookshelves and a newspaper archive.

The rooms on the first floor, which can be used for parties and meetings, are floored with wooden boards and the walls are covered with paper painted with a design, specially commissioned by the society, incorporating fragments of the society's magazine.

The end result is an exercise demonstrating a great respect for the history of the building, yet at the same time responding to the functional needs of the society which it houses.

Below, the interior of the lift which communicates the different floors of the building.

Two perspectives of the bar on the ground floor, illustrating the original design of the bar counter and the furniture. (4), (5)

A view of one of the washrooms.

Below, a view of one of the Society's work areas, located on the top floor. (6)